Instant Bargello

Susan Kisro

& COMPANY

Instant Bargello
© 2008 by Susan Kisro

That Patchwork Place® is an imprint of Martingale & Company®.

Martingale & Company
20205 144th Ave. NE
Woodinville, WA 98072-8478 USA
www.martingale-pub.com

Printed in China
13 12 11 10 09 08   8 7 6 5 4 3 2 1

Library of Congress Cataloging-in-Publication Data is available upon request.

ISBN: 978-1-56477-854-3

CREDITS

President & CEO: Tom Wierzbicki
Publisher: Jane Hamada
Editorial Director: Mary V. Green
Managing Editor: Tina Cook
Technical Editor: Robin Strobel
Copy Editor: Melissa Bryan
Design Director: Stan Green
Production Manager: Regina Girard
Illustrator: Laurel Strand
Cover Designer: Stan Green
Text Designer: Adrienne Smitke
Photographer: Brent Kane

Mission Statement

Dedicated to providing quality products and service to inspire creativity.

Contents

Introduction

Many of us are drawn to the great novelty fabrics that are so popular today. But what can we do with them? You don't want to cut them up into pieces that are too small or you will lose the character of the design. You also want to do more than simply treat a novelty print as a large center panel and add a few borders to make a quilt. You may wish to tell a story with your fabric. But, to add to the challenge, you might not have a lot of time. *Instant Bargello* can help!

As a quilt-shop owner, I began to find myself ordering many different styles of novelty prints, such as the line of Lake Superior fabrics (see page 18). I wanted to use them to their best advantage and tell a story. A bargello-like style came to mind as I started cutting strips of the fabric, creating a scene in my mind as if I were on a boat looking inland. I then sewed the strips together along their long edges, crosscut them at varying widths, and sewed them back together, staggering the rows slightly. I loved the results, as did my customers.

This simple, staggered method allows you the freedom to design the look and size of your project, whether it's a wall hanging or bed quilt. It's extremely fast and versatile, and once you've tried the Instant Bargello technique for the first time, you'll look at fabric in a whole new way.

This method is meant to be fun and artistically stimulating to quilters of all skill levels. The projects in this book are easy for kids, too! And if you have an area in your home or office where you like to display wall hangings, you can use this quick technique to create several projects to change with the seasons or holidays. The wall-hanging size also makes a perfect baby quilt.

Bargello Basics

What exactly is bargello? Bargello is a series of stacked strips set in a staggered formation.

FABRIC SELECTION

Instant Bargello is a great way to use the novelty prints that are so fun and abundant today. Many novelty prints are directional, and for these projects they work best if the design runs selvage to selvage. If the design doesn't run selvage to selvage, you must start with 1¼ yards of fabric and then cut your desired width from raw edge to raw edge. I generally use 7 to 10 fabrics for a wall hanging and 11 to 14 fabrics for a bed quilt, though your projects may vary.

Directional design runs selvage to selvage.

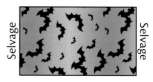

Directional design runs parallel to selvage.

You probably won't be able to find the exact fabrics that appear in the sample quilts, but that's OK. What I really want you to do is have a great time designing your own projects with fabrics of your

4

choice. Just start with a main theme print (what I call a focus print) and continue from there. The hunt for the fabrics is half the fun! Look at the projects in this book and find one in which the focus print's cut size will work for your fabric. You can then build the rest of your quilt using the project instructions. Or, study the samples to get a few ideas, and use your imagination to create a custom quilt designed by you. All samples in this book are made from quilt-shop-quality, 100%-cotton fabrics. Please support your local, independently owned quilt shop.

Your fabric should tell a story within the finished quilt. As you're choosing your fabrics, try to picture a landscape or scene in your mind. Less than half of your fabric choices should be focus prints, with these being cut considerably wider than the narrower accompanying strips. Let the design on your fabric help you decide how wide or narrow to cut your horizontal strips. For example, if you are using an outdoor scene of wilderness animals, you'll want at least one vertical repeat of the design, depending on the scale of the motif and the size of the quilt you are making (see the "Serenity" photo on page 20). Add one or two more focus prints that are on the same theme—cabins and deer in the woods, for instance. For the narrow strips, choose fabrics that help tell your story, such as bushes and pine trees. Also include some fabrics that aren't as busy, such as solids or marbled prints, to separate the scenes and give your eyes a place to rest.

Designing an Instant Bargello Quilt

If you're designing your own Instant Bargello quilt, you must allow at least 2" to 4" of additional fabric at the very top of the quilt and at the very bottom. You'll trim the top and bottom off evenly after piecing your strips together. If you're making one of the projects in this book, the extra yardage is included in the materials requirements.

One thing to consider when choosing fabrics is scale. If you keep objects at the bottom of the quilt (the foreground) proportionally larger than objects at the top (the background), you can maintain the illusion of perspective. For example, in "Harvest Hill" shown on page 16, both the pumpkin print at the bottom and the village print toward the top are large-scale prints, but the pumpkins are proportionally larger than the village. This is just how the pumpkins would appear if you were standing in the pumpkin patch—much larger than the far-off village. It will help you determine scale if you imagine yourself in the setting you're trying to create, looking toward the horizon. Imagine which things would be closest in your view and which would be farthest away.

Remember to factor in all your ¼" seam allowances when deciding on the widths of your horizontal strips. These projects contain several seams, and the inches add up in a larger quilt.

Prewashing your fabrics is a good idea. Some fabrics may have excess dye in them, especially hand-dyed fabrics, so prewashing is particularly important for those. Some fabrics may shrink slightly during the washing and drying process. Many of the fabric amounts are fairly small, so I suggest soaking them in a sink or washtub rather than washing them in a machine.

Lay your fabrics on the floor or place them on a design wall in the order pleasing to you. Step back and study your layout. When you're happy with your choices, then you're ready to begin.

Remember, you're trying to tell a story with your fabrics.

BARGELLO QUILT CONSTRUCTION

Assign each fabric a number, beginning with the fabric you want at the top of the quilt. The top strip will be fabric 1, the next strip down will be fabric 2, and so on. Use a removable blank address label or a sticky note to mark each fabric.

1. Cut the fabric strips to the width indicated in the project you're making. Trim off both selvages.
2. With right sides together, sew the fabric 1 strip to the fabric 2 strip along their long edges, using a ¼"-wide seam allowance. Press the seam allowance toward fabric 2. Add fabric 3 to the bottom of fabric 2, and press the seam allowance toward fabric 3. Continue in this

manner, adding strips and always pressing the seam allowance toward the strip you've just added.

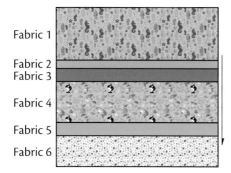

Fabric 1
Fabric 2
Fabric 3
Fabric 4
Fabric 5
Fabric 6

3. Spread out your project on a cutting mat. Don't fold your project as you're cutting the vertical rows; it must lie flat. Starting in the upper left-hand corner of the project, lay out a 24" ruler at the desired width of the first row. Cut along the long edge of the ruler. Reposition the project on the mat and continue cutting until the entire length of the row has been cut. Cut vertical rows in random widths. Suggested widths for wall hangings are 4¼", 3½", and 2¾". For the larger bed quilts, consider 6½", 5¾", and 4¼". These are only suggestions; you may cut your rows any width you want. I would caution you not to cut your rows too narrow, however, because you may not be able to recognize the design after seaming. Number the rows as you cut them, beginning with row 1 at the left. (Sewing the vertical rows together in the order you cut them will maintain continuity in the design.)

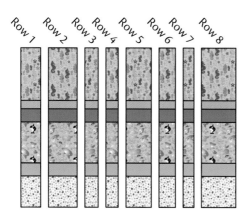

Row 1 Row 2 Row 3 Row 4 Row 5 Row 6 Row 7 Row 8

Making the Most of Fabric Motifs

You may need to cut vertical rows wider than planned if the print on the fabric requires it, such as a large building or animal that you don't want to cut down the middle.

4. Using a ¼"-wide seam allowance, sew the vertical rows together in the numbered order, staggering each row up or down by no more than 1¼" (seams should not meet). Stagger the rows randomly, not in a repetitive up-down, up-down pattern. Your project shouldn't have a uniform look; rather, it should have the effect of gently rolling terrain (see the "Lake Superior" photo on page 18). Start sewing your ¼" seams at the top of your rows. Because you pressed all the seams toward the bottom, they will lie flat as you sew one row to the next. Continue until all rows have been sewn together. Press seams to one side.

5. Trim the top and bottom of your quilt even with the shortest row.

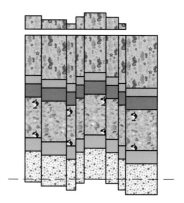

Trim even with the shortest row.

MAKING A BED-SIZED BARGELLO QUILT

It's easy to customize the size of your quilt with just a little planning. Once you understand the basic concept of this method, you can make a twin- or even king-size quilt. See "Serenity" on page 21 as a reference for making a larger quilt. Plan your design and dimensions by sketching with paper and a pencil before cutting fabric strips.

First, you'll need to determine how long you want the quilt to be. To lengthen the quilt, you can increase the width of each horizontal strip, add additional coordinating prints, or both. For a larger quilt, the horizontal strips should be in proportion to the overall size of the quilt. Focus fabrics for a bed-sized quilt should be cut into horizontal strips approximately 18" wide or at least one full vertical repeat of the design. Keep adding fabrics or increasing the width of your strips until you're satisfied with the length.

After you've cut your vertical rows and seamed them back together, your quilt top will typically be 36" to 38" wide. This will vary slightly depending on how many seams you have. If you want a twin-size quilt, make two identical strip sets and cut vertical rows from each of them. Your project will then be approximately 72" to 76" wide. For a king-size quilt, make three identical strip sets, cut the vertical rows, and then sew them together, which will yield a quilt approximately 108" to 114" wide.

Once you've determined how much fabric you need for the length of the quilt, purchase twice that amount if you want to make the quilt a twin width, or triple the amount of fabric you purchase to make the quilt a king width. It's really that simple!

Quiltmaking Basics

This section gives a brief overview of the basic skills needed to make the quilts in this book. If you're a beginner, I hope you've taken a class from your local quilt shop that introduced you to the techniques presented here. If not, I encourage you to do so. There are several good books available on quiltmaking techniques that can offer you information in detail.

ROTARY CUTTING

The first thing to do after washing and ironing your fabrics is to cut the fabrics into the appropriate strip sizes for the quilt you're making. This information is listed in the "Materials and Cutting" section of each project. When cutting the strips, follow the steps below. Left-handers should do the reverse of what they see in the illustrations.

1. Fold the fabric in half lengthwise, wrong sides together. Lay the fabric on a self-healing cutting mat with the folded edge toward you.

2. Lay a 24" ruler on the right-hand edge of the fabric. Align a horizontal line of the ruler with the folded edge of the fabric. Position the ruler only as far in from the raw edges as needed to cut through all layers of fabric. Cut along the long edge of the ruler. Always cut away from yourself. Discard the cut piece.

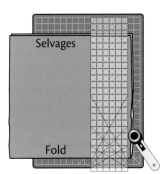

3. Rotate the fabric or mat so that the straightened edge is to your left. Measure from the straightened edge and cut a strip to the width given in the project instructions. For example, if you need a 3"-wide strip, place the 3" vertical line of the ruler on the straightened edge of the fabric. Cut along the right side of the ruler.

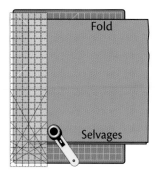

Cutting Wide Strips

If the desired width of the strip is wider than the ruler, lay the 24" ruler on the fabric. Place a smaller ruler along the left edge of the 24" ruler. Carefully move both rulers to the right until the sum of both rulers equals the desired width.

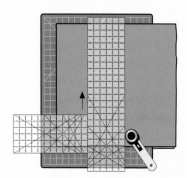

Slide the small ruler up the edge of the large ruler to check the top and bottom strip width.

MACHINE PIECING

When you sew the strips, be sure to place them right sides together and align the raw edges. It's important that all your seams measure ¼" wide. There are several ways to achieve an accurate ¼" seam. If your machine has a ¼" presser foot available, try using it. On many sewing machines, the needle position can be adjusted (refer to your manual). Or, you can use a ruler to measure ¼" to the right of the needle. Place a piece of tape or 10 to 12 sticky notes at this position and guide your fabric along it.

ADDING BORDERS

Most of the projects in this book don't include borders. However, adding one or more borders is an easy way to transform a wall hanging into a throw or lap-sized quilt. If you add a border or increase the number of borders, additional yardage for backing, binding, and batting will be required.

1. Measure the quilt top from top to bottom. Cut enough border strips to fit this measurement, piecing strips together and trimming as necessary to achieve strips of the desired length. Make two side borders.
2. With right sides together, pin the border strips to the sides of the quilt top. Using a ¼"-wide seam allowance, sew the border strips in place. Press the seam allowances toward the borders.
3. Measure the width of the quilt, including the borders just added. Make two border strips to this measurement. Sew the borders to the top and bottom edges of the quilt. Press the seam allowances toward the borders.

BACKING

Backing fabric must be at least 4" larger on all four sides than the quilt top, particularly if you take your quilt to a long-arm machine quilter. Always check with your long-arm quilter for any special requirements.

BINDING

Fabric requirements for binding listed in this book are based on using straight-grain binding strips cut 2¼" wide and stitched to the outside edges of the quilt with ¼"-wide seam allowances.

1. Cut the number of binding strips indicated in the instructions for your project. Trim off the selvages.

2. Stitch the strips together as shown to make one long strip. Trim the seam allowances to ¼". Press the seam allowances open.

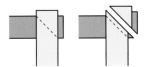 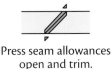

Join straight-cut strips.

Press seam allowances open and trim.

3. Press the strip in half lengthwise, wrong sides together. Press carefully, keeping the raw edges even.

4. Beginning in the middle of any side of your quilt, line up the raw edges of the binding with the edge of the quilt top. Pin the binding in place from the binding end to the first corner. Measure ¼" from the corner and mark the point with a pin as shown. Start sewing 6" from the beginning tail of your binding strip. End sewing at the pin; backstitch.

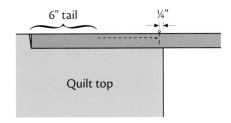

6" tail   ¼"

Quilt top

5. Turn the quilt for sewing down the next side. Fold the binding up, creating a 45° angle. Hold the fold in place, and then fold the binding back down so the edges are aligned with the quilt top as shown. Pin the binding in place, inserting another pin ¼" from the lower corner. Stitch the binding in place, beginning at the top edge and

stopping when you reach the pin at the lower corner. Repeat this process at each corner.

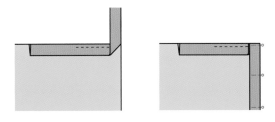

6. Stop sewing about 6" from the beginning tail of your binding strip. Trim the end tail of the binding so that it overlaps the beginning tail by 2¼".

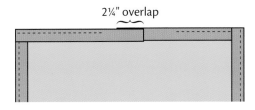

2¼" overlap

7. Open the folds of both tails and draw a diagonal line on the corner of the top binding strip. Overlap the tails, right sides together, and pin in place to secure.

8. Sew on the marked line. Check to make sure the binding fits along the unbound edge, and then trim ¼" from the stitching line. Finger-press the seam allowance open. Refold the binding in half and finish sewing it to the quilt top.

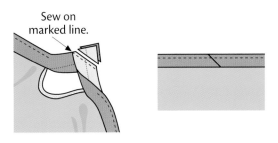

Sew on
marked line.

9. Wrap the binding over the edge of the quilt so it covers the stitching. Hand stitch the binding in place with a blind hem stitch, mitering and stitching down the corners.

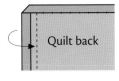 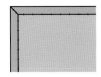

Quilt back

What young girl wouldn't enjoy this youth-sized quilt and imagine herself a friend of these fun-loving mermaids?

Merry Mermaids

Finished Size: 53" x 79½"

MATERIALS AND CUTTING

Yardages are based on 42"-wide fabrics. All measurements include ¼"-wide seam allowances.

¾ yard of mermaid print. Cut:
1 strip, 22½" x 42", for fabric 1

¼ yard of pink tone-on-tone fabric. Cut:
1 strip, 4" x 42", for fabric 2

¼ yard of purple tone-on-tone fabric. Cut:
1 strip, 6" x 42", for fabric 3

⅝ yard of sea animal print. Cut:
1 strip, 17½" x 42", for fabric 4

¼ yard of green tone-on-tone fabric. Cut:
1 strip, 6" x 42", for fabric 5

½ yard of star print. Cut:
1 strip, 13½" x 42", for fabric 6

1 yard of medium blue fabric. Cut:
6 strips, 2" x 42", for inner border
7 strips, 2¼" x 42", for binding

1⅝ yards of blue dot fabric. Cut:
8 strips, 6½" x 42", for outer border

5 yards of fabric for backing

60" x 88" piece of batting

ASSEMBLING THE QUILT

1. Sew fabrics 1–6 together in numerical order. Cut vertical rows and then sew them together, staggering each row. (Refer to "Bargello Quilt Construction" on page 5.)
2. Refer to "Adding Borders" on page 8 for instructions on sewing the inner and outer borders.
3. Layer the quilt top with batting and backing. Baste, quilt, and use the medium blue strips to bind. (Refer to "Binding" on page 9.)

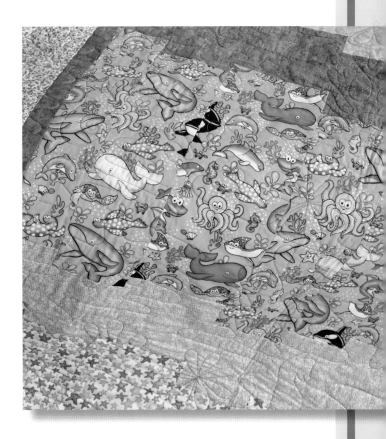

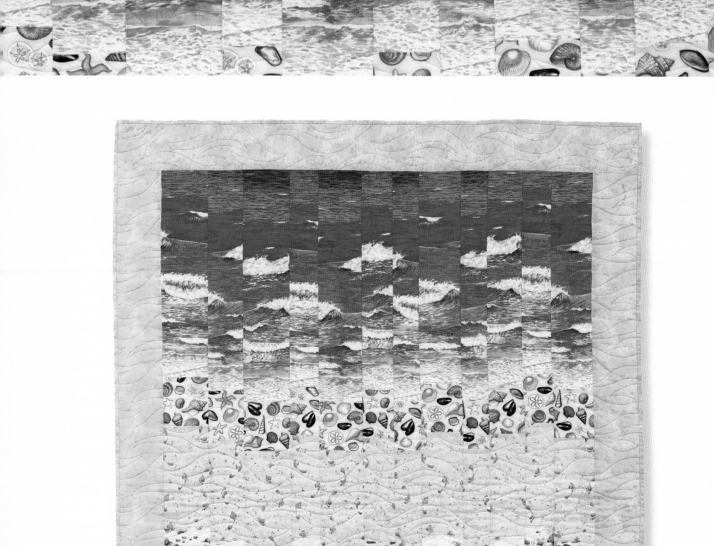

These soothing beach fabrics remind me of a special vacation my family and I spent on the tropical island of Cozumel, Mexico.

12

Footprints in the Sand

Finished Size: 44" x 60"

MATERIALS AND CUTTING

Yardages are based on 42"-wide fabrics. All measurements include ¼"-wide seam allowances.

¾ yard of water print. Cut:
1 strip, 23" x 42", for fabric 1

¼ yard of shell print. Cut:
1 strip, 4½" x 42", for fabric 2

⅓ yard of tan print. Cut:
1 strip, 9" x 42", for fabric 3

⅜ yard of beige print. Cut:
1 strip, 10" x 42", for fabric 4

½ yard of grass print. Cut:
1 strip, 13½" x 42", for fabric 5

1⅓ yards of tan tone-on-tone fabric. Cut:
6 strips, 4½" x 42", for borders
6 strips, 2¼" x 42", for binding

3 yards of fabric for backing

52" x 68" piece of batting

ASSEMBLING THE QUILT

1. Sew fabrics 1–5 together in numerical order. Cut vertical rows and then sew them together, staggering each row. (Refer to "Bargello Quilt Construction" on page 5.)
2. Refer to "Adding Borders" on page 8 for instructions on sewing the border.
3. Layer the quilt top with batting and backing. Baste, quilt, and use the tan tone-on-tone strips to bind. (Refer to "Binding" on page 9.)

Scare up some smiles from your trick-or-treaters by hanging this Halloween panel on your front door!

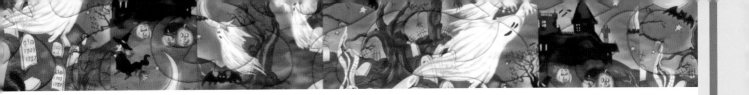

Ghosts in the Graveyard

Finished Size: 37" x 49"

MATERIALS AND CUTTING

Yardages are based on 42"-wide fabrics. All measurements include ¼"-wide seam allowances.

½ yard of bat print. Cut:
1 strip, 12" x 42", for fabric 1

⅛ yard of black solid. Cut:
1 strip, 2½" x 42", for fabric 2

⅜ yard of Halloween striped print. Cut:
1 strip, 10½" x 42", for fabric 3

¼ yard of spiderweb print. Cut:
1 strip, 6" x 42", for fabric 4

⅜ yard of ghost-and-haunted-house print. Cut:
1 strip, 11" x 42", for fabric 5

⅛ yard of green-and-blue print. Cut:
1 strip, 3" x 42", for fabric 6

½ yard of large-scale pumpkin print. Cut:
1 strip, 12" x 42", for fabric 7

⅜ yard of black fabric. Cut:
5 strips, 2¼" x 42", for binding

1⅔ yards of fabric for backing

45" x 60" piece of batting

ASSEMBLING THE QUILT

1. Sew fabrics 1–7 together in numerical order. Cut vertical rows and then sew them together, staggering each row. (Refer to "Bargello Quilt Construction" on page 5.)
2. If you'd like to increase the size of your quilt, refer to "Adding Borders" on page 8.
3. Layer the quilt top with batting and backing. Baste, quilt, and use the black strips to bind. (Refer to "Binding" on page 9.)

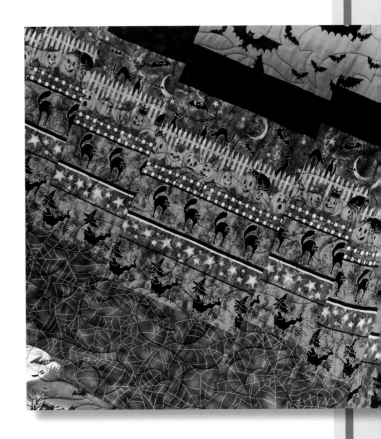

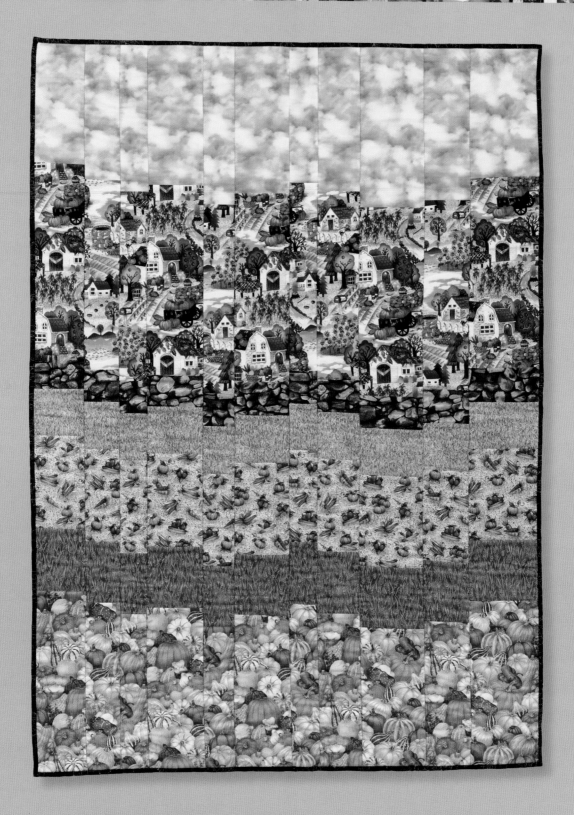

Minnesota is a burst of brilliant colors in the autumn,
making fall my favorite season of the year. Selecting
the perfect pumpkin is a family tradition.

Harvest Hill

Finished Size: 36" x 49"

MATERIALS AND CUTTING

Yardages are based on 42"-wide fabrics. All measurements include ¼"-wide seam allowances.

½ yard of blue print. Cut:
1 strip, 12" x 42", for fabric 1

½ yard of house print. Cut:
1 strip, 12½" x 42", for fabric 2

⅛ yard of rock print. Cut:
1 strip, 2¾" x 42", for fabric 3

¼ yard of green print. Cut:
1 strip, 3¾" x 42", for fabric 4

¼ yard of small-scale pumpkin print. Cut:
1 strip, 6½" x 42", for fabric 5

¼ yard of brown print. Cut:
1 strip, 4½" x 42", for fabric 6

½ yard of large-scale pumpkin print. Cut:
1 strip, 12" x 42", for fabric 7

⅜ yard of dark brown print. Cut:
5 strips, 2¼" x 42", for binding

1⅔ yards of fabric for backing

45" x 60" piece of batting

ASSEMBLING THE QUILT

1. Sew fabrics 1–7 together in numerical order. Cut vertical rows and then sew them together, staggering each row. (Refer to "Bargello Quilt Construction" on page 5.)
2. If you'd like to increase the size of your quilt, refer to "Adding Borders" on page 8.
3. Layer the quilt top with batting and backing. Baste, quilt, and use the dark brown strips to bind. (Refer to "Binding" on page 9.)

Minnesota is the "Land of 10,000 Lakes." I honor our state's heritage with this Lake Superior line of fabrics.

Lake Superior

Finished Size: 36" x 50"

MATERIALS AND CUTTING

Yardages are based on 42"-wide fabrics. All measurements include ¼"-wide seam allowances.

½ yard of blue-and-beige print. Cut:
1 strip, 12" x 42", for fabric 1

⅓ yard of leaf print. Cut:
1 strip, 8½" x 42", for fabric 2

¼ yard of gray print. Cut:
1 strip, 6¾" x 42", for fabric 3

¼ yard of green print. Cut:
1 strip, 4" x 42", for fabric 4

¼ yard of rock print. Cut:
1 strip, 5" x 42", for fabric 5

½ yard of rock-and-water print. Cut:
1 strip, 12" x 42", for fabric 6

½ yard of medium blue print. Cut:
1 strip, 12" x 42", for fabric 7

⅜ yard of gray fabric. Cut:
5 strips, 2¼" x 42", for binding

1⅔ yards of fabric for backing

45" x 60" piece of batting

ASSEMBLING THE QUILT

1. Sew fabrics 1–7 together in numerical order. Cut vertical rows and then sew them together, staggering each row. (Refer to "Bargello Quilt Construction" on page 5.)
2. If you'd like to increase the size of your quilt, refer to "Adding Borders" on page 8.
3. Layer the quilt top with batting and backing. Baste, quilt, and use the gray strips to bind. (Refer to "Binding" on page 9.)

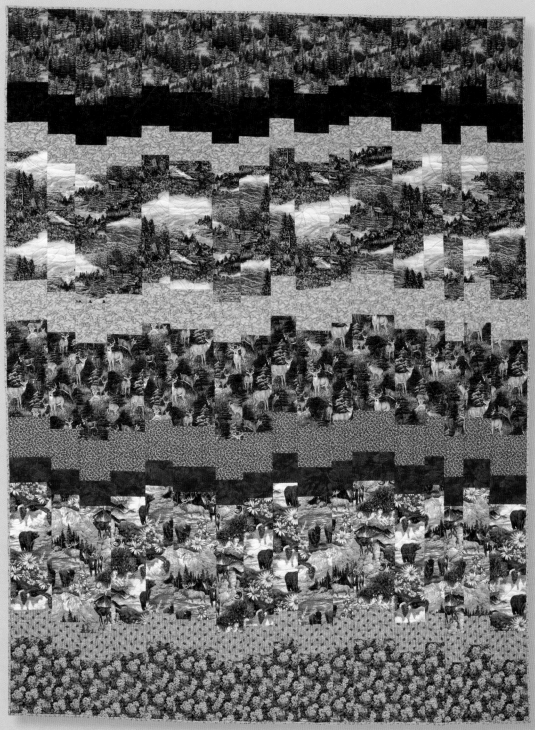

Many Minnesotans spend their vacations in a cabin
"up north." These outdoor scenes depict the natural
surroundings we enjoy in our beautiful state.

Serenity

Finished Size: 72" x 100"

MATERIALS AND CUTTING

Yardages are based on 42"-wide fabrics. All measurements include ¼"-wide seam allowances.

⅞ yard of tree print. Cut:
2 strips, 13½" x 42", for fabric 1

½ yard of dark green tone-on-tone fabric. Cut:
2 strips, 6" x 42", for fabric 2

⅓ yard of medium blue print. Cut:
2 strips, 4½" x 42", for fabric 3

1⅛ yards of deer-and-cabin print. Cut:
2 strips, 18" x 42", for fabric 4

½ yard of gold print. Cut:
2 strips, 6" x 42", for fabric 5

⅞ yard of deer-and-tree print. Cut:
2 strips, 13½" x 42", for fabric 6

½ yard of medium brown print. Cut:
2 strips, 6" x 42", for fabric 7

⅓ yard of brown tone-on-tone fabric. Cut:
2 strips, 4½" x 42", for fabric 8

1⅛ yards of bear-and-moose print. Cut:
2 strips, 18" x 42", for fabric 9

⅓ yard of leaf print. Cut:
2 strips, 4½" x 42", for fabric 10

⅞ yard of bush print. Cut:
2 strips, 13½" x 42", for fabric 11

¾ yard of tan print. Cut:
9 strips, 2¼" x 42", for binding

6 yards of fabric (or 2½ yards of 108" extra-wide fabric) for backing

90" x 108" piece of batting

ASSEMBLING THE QUILT

1. Sew one strip each of fabrics 1–11 together in numerical order. Repeat to make two identical strip sets. Cut vertical rows and then sew them together, staggering each row. (Refer to "Bargello Quilt Construction" on page 5.)
2. If you'd like to increase the size of your quilt, refer to "Adding Borders" on page 8.
3. Layer the quilt top with batting and backing. Baste, quilt, and use the tan strips to bind. (Refer to "Binding" on page 9.)

Making a King-Size Quilt

If you'd like to make a king-size quilt, increase the fabric amounts by 50% and cut three horizontal strips from each fabric. You'll make three identical sections and then sew them all together to complete your quilt. (Refer to "Making a Bed-Sized Bargello Quilt" on page 7.)

Additional Inspiration

Look at what just one focus fabric can do! I chose several coordinating fabrics with a tropical theme, and "Flamingos in Paradise" became a gift for friends in the Florida Keys.

*Clever use of a border print fabric makes "Safari Animals"
one of my favorite quilts. Most of the animal designs were
all on one piece of fabric. This quilt almost made itself!*

Acknowledgments

Thank you to:

My daughter, Ann Kisro, for your advice about putting this information together and presenting my idea to Martingale & Company.

My friend Betsy Jorgensen for your help with the bindings.

Judy Tripp for the countless hours you spent typing the manuscript, taking photographs, and always supporting me. You and Sandee Tripp are two friends I'm fortunate to have. Thank you both for your encouragement.

D. Holmes Meir Photography (www.dholmesmeir.com) for the author photo.

The staff of Martingale & Company for helping me through every step of bringing *Instant Bargello* to completion.

Special thanks to technical editor Robin Strobel for her invaluable input and excellent editing skills.

About the Author

Susan Kisro was raised in rural Minnesota, where she always enjoyed being outdoors. Growing up in the country gave her many areas to explore.

After graduating from high school, Susan began a career with the telephone company, where she remained for more than 31 years.

Shortly after retiring, Susan purchased a long-arm quilting machine. Her customers encouraged her to open a quilt shop, and after much research, The Quilting Cupboard opened in July 2003 in Rochester, Minnesota (www.thequiltingcupboard.com). Each member of her family is involved in the business. Susan's husband, Jim, was a carpenter for 30 years before becoming a certified chimney sweep. Jim is responsible for all the bookwork for the business and enjoys constructing quilt racks, rug-weaving frames, and other woodcrafts for the shop. Their daughter, Ann Kisro, is the shop manager and merchandise buyer and has the distinction of being Martingale & Company's youngest published author with her own book, *Let's Quilt!*

When possible, the Kisro family spends time relaxing on the Mississippi River. Susan continues to love the outdoors, and her appreciation of nature is reflected in the projects in this book. She hopes nature will inspire you as much as it has her.